THE POWER OF THINKING

A COLLECTION OF POEMS ABOUT HAPPINESS AND DEPRESSION IN A POSITIVE MANNER

ISHITA GOSWAMI

Made with ❤ on the Notion Press Platform
www.notionpress.com

This book is dedicated to my father Mrs. Chandan Giri who always made me happy. My English teacher Ms. Rita Bakshi always told me never to stop and practice writing every day and Ms. Vinita Roberts saw my talent for the first time and appreciated me for it. I will thank Mrs. Shashi Goswami my mother who acted as if she never understood my poems but still does. And my crazy classmates are no less than friends. They never made me feel as if I couldn't. My friend Jhalak my poet buddy

Contents

Contents

Foreword

One day at night I was listening to my sad Spotify playlist when I wrote something I never knew what was it but continued it. Everyone around me told me that the content is cringy and I won't be able to do anything but my best friend told me to try harder and harder. Also to all the young learner just like me lost in their own mind

After so many problems I faced now feel and will appreciate it for sharing with everyone reading this book.

When someone is very sad due to something continuously disturbing and mental pain is more physical, people don't cry. In the thought, *"When the pain is extreme tears dry out"*

Acknowledgements

I show my thankful gratitude to all the people who helped me endlessly working day and night for this book. And wasting their time on me efficiently. My parents for trusting me and my crazy friends for appreciating in their own wonderfyl way. I will be to thank my manager and all cordinators.

I would like to show my heartful gratitude to Ms. Gita Joshi who have always been with me through out.

1. Impossible

Just like the light of the fuse blub
Just like the sound of silence
Sometimes everything seems impossible
But sometimes just like to half make a whole
Just like two negatives make a positive
Sometimes bring happiness
Sometimes bring more then worst
But still, sometimes it seems impossible.

2. Way of light

Always stuck in the dark side
It always had a fight
It was my way to light
Sometimes it went out of sight
Sometimes it is so bright
It was my way to light
Sometimes it tore dark a part
Sometimes it was the part of the dark
It was my way to light

3. Moment that matter

It is a moment you are mine
It is a time when everything is fine
Now we will shine
Us sitting beneath the sun
Busy in your own run
But still, It is a moment you are mine
I never thought we separated
But it was always elongated
Even we are not forever
But we are still together

4. Life

Life is a grace,
But not a race
So why chase it
Life is a river
Sometimes makes us shiver
It is full of twists and turns
From this, you can never run
Sometimes brings so much of joy
So that we can enjoy

5. Mother (A tribute to my mother)

She is our homemaker
Our only caretaker
She is the bright light of our eyes
With her everything is fine
She is no less than our first teacher
She always prays for our good future
So that we can nurture
She is always bother about us
Sh is one only my mother

6. Father

The one I love
Who is always my beloved
The one who cares
With whom I never scare
The one who makes me laugh
Who is he?
The one who earns
So that we can have fun
The one who fulfills all our wish
Who is he?
My father

7. Bird

Just like a bird
I raise my wings to fly high
Out in the air
Away from fears
To raise my dreams
To leave the world behind
I raise high to the free
Just like a bird
As it wants to be like humans
To feel for life
Like the way of thinking
To spend its whole life
like the one who loves it
from the earth
I want to raise high
To feel everything
To deal with things
just like that bird

8. Time

It passes by,

just like the breeze

which never letus in ease

It flee like the birds

who are always in herds

It never stop

for rich or poor

It never takes ayone's side

It passes by just lke the breeze

Never let us in ease

It never wait

even if we are awake

Its like the uniform sea

And its calmness and motionless

It never rise or set

But we are the one who have

Learn with fun

To be like time

Keep moving on

9. Dream

We see it awake and asleep
Sometimes while sleeping
Sometimes day dreaming
We also try to reach it
Because it is our own goal
Which we focus upon
It also sometimes make as awake while sleeping
It is sometimes our own
Old cheerful or
Forceful memories
But sometimes it brings our future golries
Sometimes as dark ad brownie
It is also sometimes sweet as ice cream
It my lovely dream

10. Towards Unknown Realities

It's been years
Living away from fear
But scars are always left behind
But moments are always left behind
From glories to victories
To never-ending struggles
The things and memories stay
But the promises are forgotten forever
The reality is people won't stay
It's their job to go away

11. Faded

I am faded just a little
I am lost in the middle
I know I am losing my mind
I hated it as I need to be aided
I am the one who waited
I am faded just a little
I am a bit shaded
Because I am faded
I am also the one who
Is now afraid

12. Grandmother

Not less then my second mother
Who fights with me like
My little sister
I never leave a chance to poke
I am the one to laugh
At her every stupid joke
She is fuel of life
With her everyone
Are alive
Guess who is she
My grandmother

13. Sorrow to Happiness

That feelings which are never hidden
Just like the loosen thread
My heart was loosen too
When I was there in the dark for years away
Fears. My friends were fears
That feelings which are never hidden rise out
Just like the beautiful sun
Just like the lost fun
That feelings are which are never hidden
The worst part made me
Feel like forbidden
Just like the drops of fountain
Shining at night
Just like a thinkling
Stars bright
It was my way to happiness

14. Heart

It beats so fast
Sometimes tear us apart
But its my part
Its my heart
Its my heart
Sometimes break us so hard
Sometimes its so fake
Its my heart
which is so kind
Its always in my mind
Sometimes it rough
Sometimes it is tough to handle
But its my heart
Which beats so fast

15. Someone

Someone wake the world
So that we cam make it together
Someone motivate the world
So that we can make a motivated world
So that they can make a motive
Someone whom i want from inside
And is always sitting for my support
Someone wom i can tell
That I feel like hell
Someone about whom I wonder
Someone good in nature

16. From fear to Happiness

When tears went far
The space between heaven and hell it lie
Won't believe it die
Its fear my dear
From dizziness to never endless flight
Its our oun happiness filled with light
Just like shine of stars
Its comes with forgiveness deep inside
From deep fight to someone,s selfish motive
It all begin to be selfless right
With beautiful morning to dazzling nights

17. Friendship

From never endless fight
to never endling dancing nights
eating lots of food
alwaysseems good together
we both seem mad togehter
the best friends forever
About that person i care
with that person i never scare
We are so same
This friendship is never going to end
The person who never leaves a chance to moke
also luagh at my lame jokes
makes me more better
but never a hater

18. Success

It is a means of personal prosperity
It is the winning of leadership
Irs root lies in believe
It gives a non stressful relief
It comes from inside
full of happiness and non frustration life
It is a self freedom from worries
Its when someone access their own success

19. With Whom

On whom i rely
With whom I cry
With whom I laugh
On which I joke with
Whom I smile
On whom I trust
With whom I dream
With whom I am mad
With whom I am never sas
Wh can handle my mood swings
Who always know what I want
Who will do anything to make me smaile
With whom I moke others
With whom I never sneakthe past which never last
Who is always there to console
Who know all my secrets
With whom I never regret
Who understand when I'm in pain
Who give me

20. Family

Family is a sparkle
Just like a marble
as soft as cotton
never can be forgotten
they are going to support you at any cost
don't be lost
Family is power just like the blessing of a shower

21. Brother

You are a good brother
From whom I learn
With him had fun
He is my way to happiness
who always bother about
no one but me
he is the wise
who give me advice
to make me rise
he is no less than my second father
my all-time helper
He is my lovely brother

22. Dancers

Such a graceful dancer
who dance with passion
this possession on his head
making us all dead
this is a way of their expression
Such a great dancer
Who writes his own fate
This shows their talent
which blurts
blurt their own success and hard work

23. Teacher

She is my teacher
With all gud feature
She is my mentor
Not less then my guide
She is the one from whom i can never hide
She is a light
which makes me bright
She is my teacher
which makes us best from the rest
She is not less then our mother
She is my teacher

24. The one

The one who wants to conquer
The one who wants to glow
The one who wants to show
The one who wants to take the world together
The one whose passion never ends
The one who has only one reason
The one who was born the learn
The one who wants to earn
from the things he learns
The one who was a defeated
The one who was a loser
The one who used to get teased
The one who wants to understand
The one who wants to make things understand
The who wants to question this worthless word

25. Sister

From her, I never hide

She is my pride

With her, I always want to ride the world

My only personal makeup artist

She is my god's created stylist

She always every situation

In a manner

which makes her

my possession

She never lets me take bad decision

Her happiness

Her spark

makes my entire universe

filled with happiness

26. Following the Stars

Following the stars
On the dazzling nights
Appears as if they are going to fall as white snow
Looking for light
Something is shining brightly
Like the gold ornaments
Seems as if moving like a snail
As tiny as things that are out of sight
Forming large beautiful imaginary patterns
Sometimes a horse,
Sometimes a cat chasing a rat
As aesthetic like a artist's painting
It are the stars
Which are so far

27. Into the universe

The spark between
As if a river of light
makes me feel delighted
big circles of gas
Full of mist and smoke
Like the iron sky
Big ball fly
Into the universe
I am
A bloody ball
As hot as fire
Seems as if a soldiers standing
a bear dancing
is what I see
Into the universe
I am

28. Talking to the Moon

Dear moon
Don't go away
just stay
So that you can be the one
With whom I can have fun
with whom I can talk
With no sign of a block
Dear moon
Don't hide in the rain
Don't let me strain
Make me gain confidence
that I lost with no evidence
make me gain that confidence
that I lost with my innocence
Dear moon
Don't set by the moon
Don't Go away
just stay for a while
Don't go away miles

29. Feelings

Let's us feel
her pain
in the dark
let us make her the spark
let's make her the ray of light
always shining in the night
Let us make her the hope
Let us console her soul
Let us give her a chance
Let her give a glance
About her feelings

30. Love

It does not have a definition
it is just a perception
It is a feeling which
which have no meaning
It is dealing which
makes my healing
It can't be touch and seen
But sometimes its to much
When someone does not have anything to give
They give love
When someone does not have anything to bring
they bring love
Itt
It is just something with heart
Full of compassion and art

Vote Of Thanks

I know these days young learners are so lazy to read big stories and novels.

I just tried to make it a bit short and exciting.

Hope you won't need a dictionary.